The Joyful

With every dream, we take a chance,
A curious life, a vibrant dance.
We paint the skies with hopes anew,
In laughter's light, our spirits grew.

Exploring paths both strange and bright,
We gather moments, pure delight.
In trial and error, love will bloom,
In joy's embrace, we find our room.

A Leap Towards Light

Through shadows deep, we spread our wings,
Embracing all the joy life brings.
With faith as fuel, we soar so high,
Breaking free, embracing the sky.

The dawn whispers of hopes untold,
In every step, we forge our gold.
With hearts ablaze, we chase the day,
In a leap towards light, we find our way.

Cherished Pathways

As seasons change, we walk with care,
Through winding roads, a love we share.
In memories rich, our stories weave,
On cherished pathways, we believe.

With every step, the world unfolds,
In sunsets warm, our hearts are bold.
Together bound, through thick and thin,
On cherished pathways, we begin.

Sweet Crossroads

In the hush of twilight glow,
Dreams whisper soft and low.
Paths diverge, a choice to make,
At sweet crossroads, hearts awake.

Each step forward, fears dissolve,
In the journey, we evolve.
With courage found in tender light,
We embrace the coming night.

Blooming Possibilities

Morning dew on petals bright,
Promises of pure delight.
Every flower, a tale to tell,
In the garden, we dwell.

Colors burst in radiant show,
A world where dreams can grow.
With open hearts, we strive to see,
The blooming possibilities.

Joyful Journeys

With laughter echoing in the air,
We wander free without a care.
Every step, a new refrain,
In joyful journeys, love remains.

Stars above, they guide our way,
Lighting paths both night and day.
Together we seek and roam,
In every heart, we find our home.

The Colors of Freedom

Wings unfurl in azure skies,
Breaking chains, the spirit flies.
With every hue, a story spun,
The colors of freedom, we run.

Through fields of gold and rivers clear,
The sound of hope is all we hear.
In the tapestry of life so grand,
We stand united, hand in hand.

The Best of Both Worlds

In twilight's glow, the stars align,
Two hearts entwined, a fate divine.
Nature's whispers, city lights,
Together they dance, embracing nights.

With each breath shared, a dream unfolds,
Journeys cherished, memories told.
In every moment, love's embrace,
Two worlds in harmony, a sacred space.

Paths Paved with Smiles

Through fields of gold, we wander free,
Bright laughter carries, a sweet decree.
Hand in hand, through life we roam,
Creating joy, we build our home.

Each step we take, a story spun,
Infused with light, our hearts become one.
In every corner, warmth resides,
Paths paved with smiles, where love abides.

A Tapestry of Radiance

Colors weave in vibrant threads,
Life's tapestry, where joy spreads.
Moments glisten, laughter flows,
In this beauty, love surely grows.

Each thread a story, rich and bright,
Capturing dreams, igniting light.
Embrace the vibrant, let it be,
A tapestry of hearts, wild and free.

Savoring the Now

In quiet moments, time stands still,
Breathe in the magic, taste the thrill.
Every heartbeat, precious and rare,
Savor the now, drop all despair.

The sun dips low, the world aglow,
Each fleeting second, let it flow.
In stillness find the wonders near,
Savoring the now, hold it dear.

Heartfelt Selections

In quiet corners, memories dwell,
Whispers of stories we long to tell.
Each laugh, each tear, a thread in time,
Stitches of love, a heart's sweet rhyme.

Through winding paths of joy and pain,
We gather strength, like sun and rain.
Choices we make, with care we weave,
In heartfelt moments, we learn to believe.

With every heartbeat, a truth resides,
In shared embraces, where love abides.
Together we grow, together we stand,
In the tapestry of life, hand in hand.

Let dreams take flight on wings of grace,
In every heartbeat, find your place.
In heartfelt selections, we rise and soar,
With open hearts, we seek for more.

Joyous Detours

Life's winding trails, so full of cheer,
Lead us to places we hold dear.
Unplanned moments, a dance of delight,
In joyous detours, we find our light.

With laughter shared, our spirits bloom,
In the embrace of each vibrant room.
Chasing sunsets, beneath the stars,
In joyous detours, we heal our scars.

Every twist in the road, a chance to play,
To savor the present, come what may.
Holding hands as we laugh and glide,
In joyous detours, love is our guide.

So let us wander, let our hearts sing,
Explore the magic that freedom can bring.
In every sidestep, a story unfolds,
In joyous detours, adventure beholds.

A Symphony of Choices

In a world of noise, we find our tune,
Each note a choice beneath the moon.
Melodies merge, hearts intertwine,
In a symphony of choices, love will shine.

Pause for a moment, hear the song,
In every decision, where we belong.
With courage to step into the unknown,
In a symphony of choices, we are not alone.

Harmony woven with threads so fine,
Chords of hope and dreams align.
In every heartbeat, a rhythm flows,
In a symphony of choices, the heart knows.

Let the music guide, let your soul play,
In the dance of life, find your way.
Together we'll sing, let our voices raise,
In a symphony of choices, we embrace the days.

Serene Inspirations

In morning's light, a soft embrace,
Whispers of peace in a tranquil space.
Nature's art, a canvas wide,
In serene inspirations, we abide.

Gentle waves kiss the sandy shore,
In every breath, our spirits soar.
With every sunset, colors blend,
In serene inspirations, our hearts mend.

Silence speaks in the quiet night,
Stars above, a guiding light.
Dreams unfold in a soothing breeze,
In serene inspirations, the soul finds ease.

Let's linger here, where moments gleam,
In the tapestry of life, we weave a dream.
With open hearts, we dive within,
In serene inspirations, let the journey begin.

Sunflower Decisions

Bright petals turn to greet the sun,
In a garden where dreams run.
Choices made in the light of day,
Following the warmth, come what may.

Roots dig deep, the heart does soar,
Facing the sky, forevermore.
Each decision a seed we sow,
In the winds of fate, we let them grow.

Whimsy in the Wind

A breeze carries laughter from afar,
Whispers of joy like a shooting star.
Dancing leaves in playful delight,
Fleeting moments, hearts take flight.

Clouds drift softly, painting the sky,
Imaginary worlds where we can fly.
With every gust, new passions ignite,
In the whimsy, we find our light.

Choices that Blossom

Petals unfurl in the morning's grace,
Each choice made finds its place.
Colors vibrant, a tapestry bright,
Blooming in joy, banishing night.

With every season, new paths to see,
Life's garden, wild and free.
In the sunlight, we find our way,
Choices that blossom, day by day.

Threads of Joy

Woven with laughter, threads intertwine,
In the fabric of life, moments align.
Each connection a story told,
In the warmth of friendship, we grow bold.

Colors of hope, spun from our dreams,
In every stitch, the heart redeems.
Together we weave, a tapestry bright,
Threads of joy, shining in light.

Pathways of Promise

In the morning light we tread,
On paths where dreams are gently spread.
Each step we take, a story unfolds,
Whispers of hope in colors bold.

Beneath the trees, shadows dance,
Inviting us to take a chance.
The air is thick with sweet intent,
Guiding us where our hearts are bent.

Every turn a mystery awaits,
Unlocking doors to unknown fates.
With every breath, the world appears,
Promise blooms amidst our fears.

So let us walk with open eyes,
Embracing change, we'll rise and rise.
On pathways paved with trust and grace,
We'll find our truth, our sacred space.

Choices that Spark Joy

In every moment, choices gleam,
Like sunlight dancing on a stream.
A path to take, a door to find,
All spark the joy that fills the mind.

Pick the colors that ignite,
A canvas broad, a world so bright.
In laughter's sound, in friendships true,
Every choice leads back to you.

With every step, the heart will lift,
In simple things, we find the gift.
A gentle touch, a love's embrace,
Each choice we make leaves its trace.

So choose with heart, with open hands,
In the journey where kindness stands.
Let every moment, pure and free,
Become the joy that's meant to be.

Shimmering Opportunities

In the twilight's soft embrace,
Opportunities begin to trace.
Like stars that flicker in the night,
They whisper tales of future light.

Each shimmering chance, a fleeting spark,
Inviting us to leave a mark.
With courage found and hearts so bold,
We dive into the dreams retold.

The world expands with every choice,
In silence, we can hear their voice.
A step ahead, uncertainty comes,
But in our hearts, the answer hums.

So let us chase these lights so bright,
With open eyes, in pure delight.
For every chance that we explore,
Opens the door to something more.

The Color of Choice

Life's painted canvas, rich and wide,
Holds the colors where dreams abide.
With each decision, hues take form,
Creating magic in the norm.

The red of passion, blue of calm,
Green of growth, a soothing balm.
Yellows bright as the sun's warm smile,
In every choice, we walk a mile.

As choices blend and softly weave,
In vibrant patterns, we believe.
Each brushstroke tells a tale anew,
Of who we are, and what we do.

So paint your world with love and cheer,
Embrace the colors, hold them near.
In every choice, a life unspoiled,
In the colors of choice, we are foiled.

The Dance of Options

In twilight's glow, we stand and sway,
With choices whispering night and day.
Each step a chance, each turn a sign,
In this grand dance, our paths align.

Unfolding dreams like petals bloom,
In every corner, hope finds room.
With every heartbeat, fears dissolve,
In the embrace of what evolves.

We spin through realms both near and far,
Chasing wishes like shooting stars.
In every movement, joy unfolds,
A tapestry of stories told.

So let us twirl, let spirits soar,
In this dance of life, we'll seek for more.
With each new option, new delight,
We'll craft our fate till morning light.

Bright Horizons

Upon the dawn, the sun will rise,
With golden beams that paint the skies.
New journeys start, horizons wide,
With hope and dreams as our true guide.

Each step we take on paths unknown,
Leads to the seeds of dreams we've sown.
Together we will brave the chase,
For bright horizons, we embrace.

Through valleys green and mountains tall,
We'll lift each other, never fall.
With hearts aligned, we'll find our way,
Into the light of each new day.

So let us chase the skies so clear,
With laughter, love, and naught to fear.
For in our hearts, the truth ignites,
The promise found in bright horizons.

Embracing the Light

In shadows cast by doubts and fears,
We search for hope, we wipe our tears.
With open hearts, we seek the bright,
Embracing love, we find the light.

The warmth of dawn breaks through the gray,
Inviting us to seize the day.
With every breath, new strength we claim,
And in our souls, we'll fan the flame.

So let us dance beneath the stars,
Our spirits free, no more in bars.
In every moment, kindness shines,
With every hug, the heart entwines.

Together strong, we'll rise each time,
In unity, our souls will climb.
With open arms and a heart so free,
Embracing light, we'll simply be.

Laughter in Every Leap

With every jump, a joy we find,
In laughter's echo, hearts unbind.
We dare to dream, to take a chance,
In life's great game, we'll always dance.

From mountain tops to valleys low,
In every leap, our spirits grow.
With giggles bright and smiles wide,
We leap through life, our hearts the guide.

Through winding paths and sunlit streams,
Our laughter weaves through all our dreams.
Together we'll embrace the thrill,
With every leap, our hearts will fill.

So here's to life, to joy, to fun,
With every leap, we share the sun.
For in this journey, side by side,
There's laughter found in every stride.

Whispers of the Heart

In quiet corners where shadows play,
Soft secrets linger, gently sway.
The murmurs of hope, a tender song,
In the stillness, we find where we belong.

Dreams dance lightly on whispered sighs,
In the depths of night, they rise and fly.
With every pulse, our souls connect,
A symphony of love we can't reject.

Time drifts slowly, the world feels small,
In the echo of passions, we heed the call.
Embracing the magic, the softest glow,
Whispers of the heart, forever flow.

Choosing the Cheerful Route

Upon the road where sunshine spills,
We walk with joy, hearts full of thrills.
Laughter dances in the gentle breeze,
Finding warmth in the rustling trees.

With every step, we're light and free,
Painting our path with glee's decree.
The world around, a canvas bright,
In shades of hope, and pure delight.

Together we wander, hand in hand,
Seeking laughter in this enchanted land.
With smiles that sparkle and spirits that soar,
We choose the cheerful route forevermore.

Moments of Delight

In fleeting seconds, we often find,
The joyous treasures that life designed.
A child's laughter, a sunset's hue,
Moments of delight, sweet and true.

Sipping tea on a rainy day,
Quiet whispers in shadows play.
The warmth of hugs, a gentle kiss,
In these little things, we find our bliss.

Time pauses softly, just for a breath,
As we cherish life, defying death.
In every heartbeat, a story's spun,
Moments of delight, forever begun.

Journeys to Uplift

With every journey, we rise anew,
Exploring horizons, skies so blue.
Footprints scatter on paths unknown,
Each step a lesson, seeds are sown.

Through valleys deep and mountains high,
We chase the dreams that never die.
A tapestry woven with threads of light,
Journeys to uplift, shining bright.

In the dance with the stars, we learn to glide,
Finding strength in the changing tide.
With hearts wide open and spirits bold,
Journeys to uplift, stories untold.

Echoes of Laughter

In the garden where we played,
Sunlight danced and shadows swayed.
Whispers of joy, a gentle breeze,
Laughter ringing through the trees.

Memories etched in vibrant hues,
Childhood dreams, an endless muse.
Time may pass, but echoes stay,
In our hearts, they find their way.

With every laugh, a spark ignites,
Filling our souls with pure delights.
In the silence, we hear the sound,
Of love and joy that knows no bound.

Of laughter shared on fleeting days,
In whispers soft, the spirit plays.
Through every challenge, each small feat,
Echoes of laughter, ever sweet.

A Symphony of Selections

Notes of wisdom fill the air,
Melodies of choices rare.
In life's song, we find our part,
With each note, we weave the heart.

Chords of joy and minor strains,
Every journey, joy and pains.
In the silence, we reflect,
A symphony, we each select.

Harmony within the strife,
Crafting beauty in our life.
From the chaos, melodies rise,
An orchestra beneath the skies.

With each beat, a path unfolds,
In whispered notes, our story told.
Together, we compose the day,
In this symphony, find our way.

Moments of Exuberance

Sunrise spills on vibrant fields,
Joy in every heart it yields.
Dancing shadows, footprints made,
In these moments, no parade.

Laughter bubbles, spirits soar,
Exuberance we can't ignore.
Every heartbeat, wild and free,
Captured in this revelry.

In every glance, a spark ignites,
Filling lives with pure delights.
Seize the day, embrace the now,
Moments bold, we'll make a vow.

With open arms, we greet the dawn,
In love and laughter, we belong.
Exuberance in every hue,
Life's a canvas, bright and true.

Choices Wrapped in Light

Underneath the shining sun,
Paths diverge, our race begun.
Choices wrapped in softest glow,
In each moment, seeds we sow.

Wisdom whispers, beckons near,
Guiding us without a fear.
In the twilight, shadows dance,
Every choice, a fleeting chance.

Through the darkness, find the spark,
Illuminating every mark.
In our hands, the future gleams,
Choices shaped by all our dreams.

With courage, we embrace the light,
Navigating through the night.
Choices wrapped in love's embrace,
Leading us to a sacred space.

Echoes of Elation

In the midst of laughter's song,
Memories dance all day long.
Hearts entwined in sweet delight,
Echoes fade into the night.

Joyful whispers, soft and bright,
Carried on the wings of light.
Every moment, pure and true,
Elation shines in all we do.

The Glow of Possibility

In the dawn of brand new dreams,
Hope awakens, brightly gleams.
Endless paths begin to show,
With each step, the heart will grow.

Whispers of a world unknown,
Seeds of courage, gently sown.
Chasing stars that softly call,
The glow awaits, we risk it all.

Unfolding Wonders

Every moment, a new surprise,
Nature's beauty, vast skies rise.
Colors bloom, a vibrant scene,
Unfolding wonders, life serene.

With each breath, delicious air,
Magic hides, everywhere.
Turn the page, let stories flow,
In quiet awe, our spirits grow.

Embracing New Beginnings

A fresh start, the morning's grace,
We find hope in every place.
With open hearts, we greet the day,
Embrace the change, come what may.

The past is but a stepping stone,
Forward bound, we're never alone.
With courage deep, we set our sails,
In new beginnings, freedom trails.

The Bright Side of Deliberation

In quiet moments, thoughts unfold,
We ponder choices, brave and bold.
Each pause a gift, a chance to see,
The path ahead, where we might be.

With heart and mind in gentle sync,
We weigh the tides, and dare to think.
Sowing seeds of calm resolve,
In doubts, our strength we must evolve.

Though time may seem to slip away,
In patience lies a brighter day.
For every shadow, light will chase,
In deliberation, we find grace.

A Burst of Inspiration

A fleeting spark ignites the air,
Ideas dance, without a care.
Colors swirl, and visions bloom,
Awakening dreams from quiet gloom.

In whispers soft, the muse will call,
Encouraging the brave to sprawl.
A brush, a pen, or simple word,
From silence, magic can be stirred.

Let passion flow like rivers wide,
With open hearts, we take the ride.
For in this moment, wild and free,
A burst of life, pure creativity.

Thousand Blossoms

A garden blooms with vibrant hues,
Each petal whispers of the views.
Sunlit mornings, gentle breeze,
Nature's canvas, sure to please.

The dance of colors, rich and bright,
A symphony of pure delight.
In every bud, a story waits,
Of growth and change, of love and fates.

With every blossom, life takes flight,
In fragrant dreams that overnight.
A thousand petals, soft and fair,
Hold whispered hopes in springtime air.

Crossroads of Contentment

At forks in paths, the heart must pause,
To find what's true, to seek the cause.
In choices made, contentment lies,
Beneath the vast and endless skies.

A gentle breeze brings calm and peace,
In stillness, worries find release.
With open eyes, we see the signs,
Reflecting in our hearts, the lines.

For at these crossroads, life can shift,
A moment's thought, a precious gift.
Embracing dreams with steady hand,
We choose our path, we take a stand.

Living Colorfully

In every hue, a story shines,
Life dances bright on painted lines.
With laughter loud and spirits high,
We paint our dreams across the sky.

Emerald fields and skies so blue,
In vibrant shades, our hearts break through.
The world, a canvas, vast and grand,
We live in color, hand in hand.

Each moment's brush, a stroke of fate,
Creating memories we can't negate.
In every twist, our spirits soar,
Living colorfully, we seek for more.

So let us splash in life's embrace,
With joy and love, we find our place.
In every corner, bright and true,
We celebrate the world anew.

Kaleidoscope of Decisions

Choices swirl like colors bright,
In a kaleidoscope, they take flight.
Turning paths both far and wide,
We seek the truth with hearts as guide.

Each decision, a unique design,
Shapes our lives, both yours and mine.
In swirling patterns, futures blend,
A dance of chance that has no end.

Reflections shift with every turn,
Lessons learned and passions burn.
In the chaos, clarity found,
A symphony of dreams unbound.

So gaze within this prism clear,
Embrace the change, dismiss the fear.
With every choice, new worlds arise,
A kaleidoscope beneath the skies.

The Brilliance of Bold

To leap with courage, to stand up tall,
In the face of doubt, we give our all.
Brilliance shines in every risk,
Bold hearts know the true path brisk.

With colors vibrant, voices strong,
We march together, where we belong.
Through storms we stand, unyielding, proud,
In the heart of chaos, we speak loud.

Defying norms, we carve our way,
In brilliance bright, we choose to stay.
With every step, we write our tale,
In a world of gray, we will prevail.

So embrace the fire that burns within,
Let boldness reign, let the journey begin.
For in the end, it's love that leads,
The brilliance of bold, where the spirit feeds.

Examples of Euphoria

In laughter shared and whispered dreams,
Euphoria flows in softest streams.
The warmth of sun on skin so clear,
Moments like these draw us near.

A child's pure joy, a lover's glance,
In small delights, we find our chance.
In every hug, in every cheer,
We gather joy, we hold it dear.

From mountain peaks to ocean waves,
Euphoria calls, our spirit saves.
In fleeting seconds, here we stand,
In simple kindness, heart in hand.

So let us seek those precious days,
In shared smiles and loving ways.
For euphoria, a timeless thread,
Weaves all our moments, love ahead.

Trails of Cheer

Through the woods we wander free,
Laughter dancing near a tree.
Sunlight kisses every leaf,
Joyful moments, pure belief.

Mossy paths beneath our feet,
Nature hums a tune so sweet.
Whispers carried on the breeze,
Filling hearts with gentle ease.

Colors splash on every side,
In this haven, we confide.
Every smile, a step we take,
On this trail, no heart can break.

As the sunset paints the sky,
We share dreams that soar and fly.
Hand in hand, we'll journey far,
Guided by our shining star.

Choosing the Radiant Route

At the fork, we pause and think,
Two paths meet where shadows sink.
One is dark, the other bright,
Choosing warmth, we seek the light.

With each step, the sunshine beams,
Filling hearts with hopeful dreams.
Golden rays on faces shine,
In this space, all souls align.

Birds are singing, skies are clear,
Every heartbeat brings us near.
In the glow of love's embrace,
We find strength in every place.

Through the fields of bright delight,
Joy is ours, with hearts so light.
Together on this radiant route,
Every choice, we'll not doubt.

Hearts in Bloom

In the garden, petals spread,
Colors vibrant, love is fed.
Each bloom whispers tales of grace,
In this world, we find our place.

Butterflies dance in the air,
Softest fragrance everywhere.
Sunshine warms the tender shoots,
Nature's orchestra, our roots.

Moments shared beneath the sky,
Hearts in bloom as time floats by.
Watered with affection's care,
Growing strong, beyond compare.

Seasons change, yet we remain,
Bound by love, through joy and pain.
In this garden, side by side,
Forever is our gentle guide.

Quiet Revelations

In the silence, thoughts arise,
Whispers soft, like lullabies.
In still waters, truths unfold,
Magic found in moments bold.

With the dawn, the world awakes,
Mysteries in quiet stakes.
Every heartbeat brings new sight,
In the calm, we find the light.

Glimpses of what's yet to be,
In the stillness, we are free.
Listening close, we'll understand,
Life's sweet secrets, hand in hand.

So we gather, and we share,
Moments show how much we care.
In reflections, wisdom shines,
Quiet revelations, love defines.

The Gift of Tomorrow

In the dawn's embrace, a new day breaks,
Whispers of hope in the sunlight wakes.
Promises linger in the air, so bright,
Gift of tomorrow, a wondrous sight.

With each step forward, dreams take flight,
Casting away shadows, embracing light.
Possibilities bloom like flowers in spring,
The heart dances, ready to sing.

Yesterday's burdens, cast aside with care,
Tomorrow's canvas calls, waiting to share.
Threads of our stories weave through the night,
A tapestry rich in colors so bright.

So cherish each moment, let love be the guide,
In the dance of the future, let joy decide.
Together we wander, hand in hand we roam,
In the gift of tomorrow, we find our home.

Flourishing Decisions

In the garden of choices, seeds we sow,
Watered with wisdom, they start to grow.
Branches of life stretch, reaching for skies,
Each decision made holds a sweet surprise.

With courage we step, into the unknown,
Nurtured by hope, our spirits have grown.
Paths may diverge, yet still we remain,
In the cultivation, we banish the pain.

Sunshine of laughter, shadows of doubt,
Through the storms of life, we muster a shout.
Flourishing hearts, in the field of fate,
Embrace the journey, it's never too late.

So tend to your choices, let passion ignite,
With every new dawn, our futures take flight.
In the essence of growth, we draw ever near,
Flourishing decisions, our vision is clear.

Finding Gold in the Ordinary

In the simple moments, treasures reside,
Whispers of beauty in the daily tide.
A smile shared, a laugh on the street,
Finding gold in the ordinary, pure and sweet.

The rustle of leaves, a soft morning breeze,
Patterns of life create a gentle ease.
In the mundane, magic begins to unfold,
Each day a new story waiting to be told.

Sunlight peeking through the window pane,
Comfort in the rain, joy in the pain.
In quiet corners, wonders are found,
Finding gold in the ordinary, rich and profound.

So pause and reflect, let your heart align,
In every small thing, divinity shines.
Embrace the mundane, let your spirit soar,
For in life's simplicity, we find so much more.

Sweet Serendipity

In the twist of fate, a chance encounter calls,
Moments unexpected can break down the walls.
Like raindrops in sunshine, a dance so free,
Sweet serendipity, come dance with me.

Paths cross like rivers, in wild, gentle ways,
Leading us onward through bright, tangled days.
Magic unfolds in the blink of an eye,
Sweet serendipity, let our spirits fly.

With laughter as music and hope as our guide,
We navigate life with hearts open wide.
Each little surprise, a spark in the dark,
Sweet serendipity, igniting the spark.

So trust in the journey, let go of the plan,
In each twist and turn, find your own span.
For in life's surprises, pure joy we'll see,
In sweet serendipity, just you and me.

Graceful Divergences

Paths unfold in quiet grace,
Whispers turn to gentle trails.
In the dance of fate we trace,
Choices woven, timeless tales.

In the pause of dusk's embrace,
Stars align in twinkling skies.
Every step a soft embrace,
Life's adventure never lies.

With each turn, a lesson learned,
Moments catch like fleeting light.
Hearts ignite as passions burn,
In the shadows, hopes take flight.

Though the roads may twist and bend,
Every journey finds its way.
In the end, each path we tend,
Gives us strength for a new day.

Shimmering Opportunities

Glistening dreams in morning dew,
Whispers echo all around.
Every chance, a vibrant hue,
Floating softly, hope is found.

In the garden of our minds,
Seeds of courage take their turn.
Blooming bright, our spirit binds,
For new heights, we fiercely yearn.

Moments spark like fireflies,
Lighting paths both near and far.
In our hearts, no need for sighs,
Shimmering like a guiding star.

Every choice, an open door,
Inviting joy to fill the air.
Step ahead, let dreams explore,
In these chances, we declare.

The Melody of Authorship

Pen in hand, the canvas bare,
Words like rivers flow and twine.
Crafting worlds beyond compare,
Every line a subtle sign.

In the quiet, voices sing,
Stories rise like morning light.
Through the heart, the echoes ring,
In creation, pure delight.

Characters in vibrant stride,
Weaving tales that stir the soul.
Adventures waiting to collide,
As we journey to our goal.

Every chapter tells our truth,
Ink and paper, life combined.
In the scribbles of our youth,
The melody we leave behind.

Choices that Sing

Every choice a note we play,
Harmonies that lift the heart.
In the light of dawn's soft ray,
Life's sweet rhythm finds its start.

With each turn, a chance unfolds,
Magical in every guise.
Stories waiting to be told,
In the mirror of our eyes.

In the dance of dreams and fate,
We embrace both joy and fear.
Every path we navigate,
Brings us closer, year by year.

Choices echo, bold and bright,
Resonating deep within.
In the shadows of the night,
Every whisper, let it spin.

Calm in the Chaos

In the midst of swirling storms,
A gentle voice breaks the norm.
Breathe in peace, let go of strife,
Find the stillness, embrace life.

Winds may howl, and shadows play,
But there's a light that guides the way.
Close your eyes, feel the ground,
In chaos, calm can be found.

Every heartbeat, a steady drum,
In the chaos, peace will come.
Hold on tight, don't drift away,
The heart knows how to stay.

As the world spins wild and free,
Seek the quiet, you will see.
In the eye of the storm, there's grace,
Calm in the chaos, a sacred space.

A Constellation of Choices

Stars shine bright in endless night,
Each decision a guiding light.
Paths diverge, our futures weave,
In the night sky, we believe.

A flicker here, a glimmer there,
Each moment held with tender care.
What we choose shapes who we are,
A constellation, near and far.

In the face of doubt and fear,
Choices spark a vision clear.
Step by step, we find our way,
Crafting dreams from a single ray.

With every choice, a tale unfolds,
A map of hearts, adventures bold.
Trust the stars, they light your flight,
In the dark, they shine so bright.

Journeying into Joy

With each step, the world unfolds,
A tapestry of stories told.
Laughter dances on the breeze,
Joy in moments, simple, free.

Through valleys deep and mountains high,
Chasing dreams that touch the sky.
Bask in sunlight, feel the glow,
Journeying where the wild winds blow.

Find the joy in every stride,
In the heart, let love reside.
Each turn holds a gift unseen,
In the journey, joy is gleaned.

Embrace the road, wherever it leads,
Nurture the heart, plant joyful seeds.
For life's a dance, a sweet deploy,
Step by step, journey into joy.

The Path of Light

Beneath the canopy of stars,
A journey waits with open arms.
Footsteps whisper tales of old,
Each step a spark, a story told.

Through shadows dense, a lantern glows,
The heart ignites where courage flows.
With every turn, the spirit takes flight,
Following the echoes of pure light.

Winding paths of faith and grace,
Lead us onward, a sacred space.
In the hush of night, we find our way,
Together we chase the dawn of day.

Hope and dreams entwined as one,
Underneath the watchful sun.
The path is bright with love's embrace,
A journey shared, a wondrous place.

A Canvas of Delight

Brush in hand, colors abound,
Each stroke a joy waiting to be found.
A canvas blank, inviting grace,
With every hue, the heart finds its place.

Splashes of laughter, strokes of cheer,
Painting memories we hold so dear.
Vivid shades that dance in light,
Creating a world both bold and bright.

In the warmth of sunlit days,
Art unfolds in myriad ways.
A masterpiece born from simple glee,
A canvas alive, wild and free.

As colors merge, the spirit sings,
A celebration of all good things.
In each creation, hearts unite,
Together we share this canvas of delight.

The Charm of Brave Choices

With every choice, a path unfolds,
A tale of courage, waiting to be told.
Step forward, heart alight,
Discovering realms beyond the night.

Whispers of doubt may cloud the mind,
Yet in these moments, strength we find.
For bravery blooms in the face of fear,
A garden of hope, bright and clear.

Each decision, a turning point,
An invitation to boldly anoint.
With open arms, we embrace our fate,
Creating a life, rich and great.

The charm lies in the risks we dare,
In every journey, love's sweet care.
Embrace the unknown, let your heart rejoice,
For life is a dance of brave choices.

Spirited Embraces

In the soft glow of twilight's grace,
Hearts entwine in a warm embrace.
Laughter dances on the breeze,
A spirited joy that brings us ease.

With open hearts, we share this space,
Where love and friendship find their place.
In every hug, a tale unfolds,
A bond like magic, cherished and bold.

Through trials faced, we stand as one,
Together we shine, brighter than the sun.
In every moment, grace we trace,
Finding comfort in each embrace.

So let us weave a tapestry fine,
Of spirited love, forever entwined.
In this dance of life, let's celebrate,
The warmth of each other, we cultivate.

Serendipitous Steps

In a garden where wildflowers bloom,
Each petal whispers secrets of fate.
Beneath the trees, laughter finds room,
A chance encounter, a twist of state.

Paths crossed under a sky so wide,
With every turn, joy unfolds anew.
Hearts dance lightly, side by side,
In the hands of time, their dreams brew.

Footprints linger on this soft ground,
Echoes of laughter and stories shared.
In serendipity, true love is found,
A testament to the moments they dared.

As twilight descends with a gentle sigh,
Memories weave in a silken thread.
Through shadows and light, their spirits fly,
Serendipity guides where they are led.

Sunlit Decisions

Beneath a sky painted gold and blue,
Choices unfold like petals in spring.
With each dawn, a chance to renew,
In the warmth of light, our hearts take wing.

Paths diverging in the soft light,
Each step taken, a song to create.
With courage found in the bright sight,
Sunlit decisions shape our fate.

Moments glitter like dew on the grass,
As the day blooms with vibrant hues.
In the present, futures gently pass,
Casting aside the doubts we lose.

With every heartbeat, a story unfurls,
Creating memories that softly flow.
In the sunlit embrace, our vision twirls,
Guided by light to where dreams grow.

Radiant Turns

In the stillness of the morning light,
Choices shimmer like diamonds on dew.
Each radiant turn, a path ignites,
Promising dreams that feel so true.

With gentle whispers, the heart will steer,
Lost in the beauty of what could be.
Embracing the moments we hold dear,
Radiant turns lead us to be free.

Winding roads where wishes reside,
In the dance of time, we lose our fears.
In every twist, love becomes our guide,
In the laughter shared, we find our cheers.

Through the seasons, our journey flows,
Every turn an echo of bright desire.
In the warmth of connection, love grows,
United together, we rise higher.

Whispers of Delight

In twilight's glow, soft secrets sing,
Whispers of delight float through the air.
With every breeze, our souls take wing,
In the dance of night, we find our pair.

Stars shine bright in a velvet sky,
Stories woven with threads of delight.
In silent moments, as time slips by,
Hearts beat softly, wrapped in the night.

Magic lingers in every shared glance,
Each smile a promise that the heart keeps.
In the stillness, we find our chance,
Whispers of love in the dreams that seep.

As dawn breaks, painting skies anew,
The echoes of delight will stay near.
In every moment, forever true,
Love's tender whispers, soft and clear.

Blessings in the Balance

In quiet moments, we find our grace,
The gentle whispers of love's embrace.
Counting the gifts, both big and small,
In the balance of life, we find it all.

Through trials faced, we grow so bold,
With wisdom gained, our hearts unfold.
Each step measured, with care we tread,
In the dance of fate, the path we thread.

The laughter shared, the tears we've shed,
In every heartbeat, the life we've led.
For blessings come in every shade,
In shadows cast, the light cascades.

And as we walk this winding road,
With open hearts, our stories flowed.
Together we balance, rise, and fall,
In love's embrace, we have it all.

The Joyful Navigator

With compass set, we chart our course,
Through waves of change, we find our source.
The stars above, a guiding hand,
In every journey, hope will stand.

Across the seas, our spirits soar,
In every harbor, we seek for more.
The winds may shift, yet we remain,
True to our dreams, through joy and pain.

With laughter loud and hearts aglow,
We navigate where wild winds blow.
In unison, we sing our tune,
Underneath the watchful moon.

The tide may rise, but so do we,
In every moment, pure and free.
Together, we voyage hand in hand,
The joyful navigator, we'll take a stand.

Abundant New Beginnings

In dawn's first light, the world awakes,
With every heartbeat, a chance that makes.
Embrace the fresh start, let go of the past,
For life's a journey, vast and fast.

Through fields of dreams, we wander wide,
Every moment a wave, a rolling tide.
With open arms, we greet the day,
In abundant beginnings, we'll find our way.

The sun will rise, chasing night away,
With colors bright, it paints our stay.
In storms we gain strength, through laughter we grow,
In every new chapter, love will flow.

So take a breath, let your spirit sing,
In the dance of life, we're everything.
With hearts aligned to a chorus sweet,
Abundant beginnings, our journey's beat.

Embracing Tomorrow's Sun

With every dawn, a promise made,
In golden hues, all doubts will fade.
We rise anew, with hope in sight,
Embracing tomorrow, a warm delight.

The shadows linger, but we stand tall,
In fields of dreams, we heed the call.
With open hearts, we face the morn,
For in each challenge, new strength is born.

The whispering breeze, a gentle guide,
As we walk forward, side by side.
With every step, the future gleams,
In love and laughter, we weave our dreams.

So let us bask in the sun's embrace,
In the dance of life, we find our place.
With every heartbeat, we shall run,
Embracing the warmth of tomorrow's sun.

Bright Paths Ahead

In the morning glow we rise,
With dreams that stretch across the skies.
Each step a promise, each breath a chance,
Hope ignites our bold advance.

Winding trails through fields so wide,
Inviting us to take the ride.
With laughter echoing through the air,
We chase the light without a care.

Mountains high and valleys low,
Together we will learn and grow.
With every sunrise comes a way,
To find our strength in light of day.

The road ahead, it calls us near,
With every turn, we shed our fear.
A journey rich with tales to share,
Bright paths await, if we just dare.

The Joy of Decision

In moments still, we weigh our choice,
Listening closely to our inner voice.
A path unfolds, both bright and new,
With every step, our hearts break through.

Choices glimmer like stars at night,
Guiding us toward the dawning light.
With open minds, we'll find our way,
In courage, we will not delay.

Turning points in life so grand,
With dreams alive, united we stand.
Each decision leads us to unfold,
A tapestry of stories told.

The joy resides in paths we take,
In every chance, new ground we break.
With hearts aligned and spirits free,
Decision's joy, our destiny.

Sunlit Options

Sunlit paths stretch far and wide,
Inviting us with arms open wide.
A world of choices, bright and clear,
Every turn brings something dear.

Golden rays paint the day so bright,
Each shadow holds a secret light.
Hope blooms gently in the air,
As we embark without a care.

With every glance, new dreams arise,
A canvas fresh beneath the skies.
Paths to take, and roads to see,
In sunlit options, we find glee.

Together we will venture forth,
Embracing every place of worth.
With hands entwined, we'll face the sun,
In choices made, our joy's begun.

Embracing the Green Light

As the signal shines, we feel the spark,
Opportunities beckon from the dark.
With hearts aligned, we take our cue,
The green light glows, inviting you.

Forward we go, with dreams in hand,
Together weaving futures grand.
In every moment, bold and bright,
We trust the journey, guided by light.

The thrill of choice, it fills the air,
With open hearts, we show our care.
In every decision, pathways share,
A vibrant life, beyond compare.

Embracing change, our spirits soar,
In this great dance, we seek for more.
With every step, we find our way,
Embracing the green light of today.

Serendipitous Turns

In shadows where the wanderers tread,
Whispers of fate linger, softly said.
A path obscured, yet brightly so,
Each step unfolds a tale to bestow.

Lost in the maze of life's grand design,
Chance encounters intertwine, align.
With every twist, a spark ignites,
Guiding hearts through starry nights.

In laughter shared beneath the moon's gaze,
Synchronicities weave through the haze.
The magic of moments, ever rare,
Serendipity breathes in the air.

So trust the journey, let go of the helm,
In life's canvas, you are at the realm.
With open arms, embrace what you find,
Serendipitous turns, the heart's sweet bind.

Delight in Every Step

On cobblestones kissed by morning light,
Each footfall dances, spirits take flight.
A melody hums through the bustling street,
Delight wraps around where new souls meet.

With laughter ringing in the cool air,
Moments unfold like petals, so rare.
Sipping the nectar of everyday bliss,
Finding the joy in the simple kiss.

Colors burst forth in vibrant array,
Life paints a canvas in hues of the day.
In every whisper of wind on your face,
Delight in each step becomes a warm embrace.

So wander boldly, let your heart lead,
In each little gesture, plant kindness's seed.
In this journey, your spirit will soar,
Delight in every step, forevermore.

Radiant Possibilities

In the dawn's glow, dreams take their flight,
With wings made of hope, they aim for the light.
Each moment, a canvas awaiting the brush,
Radiant possibilities in life's gentle hush.

With hearts open wide, we sculpt our fate,
Building bridges that none can abate.
Every heartbeat a drum, echoing strong,
In the symphony's chorus, we all belong.

Layers unveil as we venture and seek,
The beauty of boldness, it's never too meek.
Through struggles and triumphs, we carve our way,
Radiant possibilities bloom day by day.

So let go of doubt, let your spirit aspire,
Fan the flames of your heart's pure desire.
In the tapestry we've yet to unfurl,
Radiant possibilities shape our world.

The Dance of Selection

In the ballroom of choices, we twirl and sway,
Each decision a partner in life's grand ballet.
With each whispered option, we ponder, we weigh,
The dance of selection leads us on our way.

With grace, we navigate the intricate floor,
Where paths intertwine, and we seek to explore.
A step toward the future, a glance to the past,
The rhythm of choices unfolds, unsurpassed.

Moments of courage, whispers of doubt,
In this dance of life, we learn what it's about.
To follow our instincts, embrace the unknown,
The beauty of selection is how we've all grown.

So twirl with abandon, let your heart lead,
In the dance of selection, find what you need.
For every choice made, a story unfurls,
In the dance of life's wonder, we twirl through the worlds.

A Glimmering Compass

In the twilight, a compass glows,
Pointing to dreams that nobody knows.
It whispers softly, of paths untrod,
Guiding the heart, beneath the façade.

With each spin, a story unfolds,
Of courage found, and secrets told.
The north star winks above the trees,
As hope ignites upon the breeze.

Through valleys deep, and mountains steep,
The compass leads, the soul to keep.
In the journey, joy resides,
In every step, where love abides.

So follow the glimmer, let it ignite,
Your dreams alight in the darkest night.
For within each twist, a promise lies,
A glimmering compass guides the wise.

The Treasure of Today

Each moment holds a golden key,
Unlocking doors, setting us free.
With laughter shared and stories spun,
The treasure of today has just begun.

In simple joys and smiles bright,
In the warm embrace of fading light.
There lies a wealth that time can't steal,
In every heartbeat, we truly feel.

The past may fade, the future's unsure,
But today is ours, a gift so pure.
So gather close, let worries sway,
Discover the treasure found today.

In memories made and love that's shown,
In every kindness, we have grown.
Hold dear this moment, come what may,
For life's true bounty is in today.

Embrace Your Whims

Dance in the rain, let laughter soar,
Whisk away worries, open the door.
For whims are whispers that beckon the soul,
Inviting you gently to lose control.

In fleeting moments, creativity gleams,
Follow your heart, pursue your dreams.
Chase the shadows with colors bright,
Embrace your whims, for they bring delight.

Let spontaneity guide your way,
In secret gardens where children play.
The world is vast, a canvas wide,
So splash it with joy, let your heart decide.

For life's best tales are often spun,
In playful whims, in laughter, in fun.
So take the leap, let go of the reins,
Embrace your whims, break free of the chains.

The Delightful Unknown

In the folds of time, mysteries lie,
Whispers of dreams that beckon the sky.
With every step, adventure awaits,
In the delightful unknown, where fate creates.

The shadows dance, inviting the brave,
To seek the wonders, the paths we crave.
With courage held close, we venture forth,
Into the magic, of untold worth.

The heart takes the lead, the mind lets go,
Uncharted waters, a vibrant flow.
In the delightful unknown, we find our song,
Where every soul feels they truly belong.

So breathe in the thrill, let curiosity guide,
In the realms of wonder, there's nothing to hide.
With open arms, let life be shown,
The beauty revealed in the delightful unknown.

Your Smile

Your smile lights up the night,
A beacon shining bright.
It warms my tired soul,
And makes the shadows whole.

In every curve, I see grace,
The softness of your face.
A gentle spark of cheer,
Banishing the fear.

When laughter dances free,
You're the magic key.
Unlocking joy so deep,
In memories we keep.

So hold that smile up high,
Like stars that fill the sky.
For in its simple glow,
Together we will grow.

My Compass

In every storm I find,
You're the guiding mind.
A steady hand to hold,
Through warmth and through cold.

When pathways twist and turn,
Your light is what I yearn.
With you, I can be brave,
Together we will save.

Your wisdom, soft and clear,
Reminds me to have cheer.
With every choice we make,
Our bond will never shake.

So let us boldly roam,
With love, we find our home.
Each step that we embrace,
With you, I feel the grace.

Tapestry of Bliss

Each thread a story shared,
Woven with love, we dared.
In colors bright and bold,
A warmth against the cold.

The laughter in each stitch,
Brings joy, a loving witch.
With every gentle pull,
Our hearts become more full.

Through trials, we unite,
Creating pure delight.
In this fabric divine,
Your heart entwines with mine.

Together, we'll explore,
This tapestry and more.
A journey we can't miss,
In our thread of bliss.

Joyful Paths

We wander side by side,
With hearts both open wide.
On paths where flowers bloom,
Dispelling all the gloom.

Each step a dance we share,
In moments rich and rare.
With laughter as our song,
In this place we belong.

Through sun-kissed fields we roam,
Where every turn feels home.
In shadows and in light,
We'll chase the stars at night.

So hand in hand we'll go,
Through valleys high and low.
For every joyful path,
Creates our perfect math.

The Art of Choosing Bliss

In every choice we face,
We carve our sacred space.
With love as our intent,
The joy is always sent.

Through trials we may tread,
In light we'll be led.
For in each gentle sigh,
We learn to laugh and fly.

The art of joy unfolds,
As life's true story molds.
With gratitude in heart,
We'll never be apart.

So let us paint the day,
In colors bright and gay.
For choosing bliss is wise,
Together, we will rise.

The Heart's Canvas

Colors blend in soft embrace,
Each stroke a memory, a trace.
Whispers of love upon the page,
A masterpiece born, free from cage.

Shadows dance in twilight glow,
Eager hearts begin to flow.
Canvas wide with dreams untold,
In every hue, our stories hold.

Brush of hope, a gentle hand,
Creating visions, vast and grand.
In every corner, bright and bold,
The heart's true art will soon unfold.

In silence, feelings start to speak,
Through palettes rich, we find the peak.
Bold and tender, let it be,
The canvas breathes, reflecting me.

Blossoms of Intention

In the garden, seeds we sow,
With gentle care, we watch them grow.
Each blossom bright, a wish unfurled,
In vibrant hues, they greet the world.

Morning dew on petals gleam,
Whispers carried on the stream.
Intentions bloom with every ray,
A fragrant start to each new day.

In every bud, a tale begins,
Stories woven through life's spins.
Through seasons change, they flourish bright,
A tapestry of pure delight.

With open hearts, we greet the morn,
In every bloom, a dream reborn.
Together we shall tend and share,
Blossoms of love, with utmost care.

Radiance in the Skies

Glistening stars in velvet night,
Softly whispering dreams in flight.
Moonbeams dance on quiet seas,
A canvas wrapped in tranquil ease.

Clouds drift by, a painted scene,
Hues of orange, pink, and green.
Hearts awaken to nature's call,
Under the spell of twilight's thrall.

Constellations guide our way,
Through endless wonder, night and day.
In every glance, a story deep,
Radiance found where shadows creep.

So lift your gaze, embrace the glow,
Let every heartbeat feel the flow.
In skies adorned, our spirits soar,
Together, we are forevermore.

Laughter in the Air

Echoes of joy, a vibrant sigh,
Laughter dances, soaring high.
Children play in fields so wide,
Each giggle a wave, a joyful tide.

Bubbles rise in playful cheer,
Floating dreams that seem so near.
Tickles shared on sunny days,
Laughter weaves through life's sweet maze.

In every chuckle, memories bloom,
Filling hearts, dispelling gloom.
With each shared smile, burdens lift,
Laughter, love's most precious gift.

So gather close, let spirits blend,
In laughter's light, let hearts transcend.
Together, we'll create a song,
In laughter's arms, we all belong.

Reveling in Possibility

Each dawn brings hope anew,
Whispers of dreams yet to unfold.
With open hearts, we pursue,
Paths of stories yet untold.

In the garden of our mind,
Seeds of courage start to grow.
With every chance we find,
Wonders await, as we sow.

Tides of Elation

The waves crash with delight,
Laughter dances in the air.
Underneath the moonlit night,
Joyful hearts know no despair.

As the stars begin to sing,
We surrender to the flow.
Embracing what life can bring,
Riding high, we let it go.

Heartfelt Dilemmas

In the silence of the night,
Choices linger, shadows play.
What feels wrong can seem so right,
Guiding us along the way.

Echoes of a love once near,
Pull us back to where we stood.
Amidst joy, we feel the fear,
Searching for a greater good.

Chasing Elective Sunbeams

In the soft light of the morn,
We chase dreams across the sky.
With each step, we are reborn,
Radiant hopes that never die.

Through the laughter and the tears,
We journey where the heart leads.
Collecting moments, thoughts, and fears,
Planting love like scattered seeds.

Milton Keynes UK
Ingram Content Group UK Ltd.
UKHW020739071024
449371UK00014B/953